Tad! or, The Frog Prince
By James Mainard O'Connell

LICENSING & PRODUCTION INQUIRIES
Uproar Theatrics, LLC.
hello@uproartheatrics.com | www.UproarTheatrics.com

Tad! or, The Frog Prince copyright © 2023 by James Mainard O'Connell

Tad! or, The Frog Prince is published by Uproar Theatrics, LLC
500 8th Ave FRNT 3, #1714 New York, NY 10018

ISBN: 978-1-968051-12-9

First Printing, April 2025

The shorter, 5-8 actor version of *Tad! or, The Frog Prince* was originally produced by Golden Duck Productions as a touring show in October and November, 2006 in and around Staunton, VA. It was directed and designed by playwright James Mainard O'Connell and produced by Mark Mannette.

The cast was:
Sarah E. Bentley
Evan Crump
J.E. Knowlton
Julie E. Roundtree
Harper York

The longer version of *Tad! or, The Frog Prince* was originally produced by Episcopal Collegiate School in Little Rock, AR in January, 2022. It was directed by Katie Greer and designed by playwright James Mainard O'Connell.

The cast was:
Anna Russell Brantley
Matthew Collins
Lucy Coon
Will Davis
Charlie Johnson
Arden Jones
Julia Krowski
Claire Lammers
Weston Leacock
Toni Little
Emma McGraw
Juliana Neesvig
Kai Nayles
Lili Norman
Cameron Pace
Hattie Paul
Izabella Pumphrey
Zoe-Olivia Spencer
Spurlock
Allison Tuite
Hali Tucker

The technical crew was:
Victoria Bravo-Bowles
Gloria Calhoun
Madison Johnson
Ann Katz
Ryan Utecht
Tate Mikles
Mckenzie Riley
Marek Sewell
Olivia Tulgetske
Annie West
Oliver Wippo
Madison Zamilpa

Time:
Once upon one.

Setting:
The Royal Castle. The Royal Wood. The Royal Pond.

Characters:
Tad – The Prince (20s)
Ernest – The other Prince (20s)
Sylvia – The Princess (20s)
Fred – Tad's Servant (20s)
King - The King (so very old)
Peasant - A Peasant (any age)
Phil - An Old Guard (so very old)
Healer - A Healer (old, but not so old)
Marge - A Fellow Healer (old, but not so old)
Helen – A Peasant (20s)
Witch – A Witch (who even knows?)
Guard 1 (aka Mildred) – A Guard (20s)
Guard 2 – Another Guard (older than Guard 1)
Lady Frog – A Frog, who is also a lady (20s)
Rabbit - A Rabbit (how old do rabbits get?)
Protestors - Three or more (any age)
Fish – A Fish, or several of them (see Rabbit)
Audience Leaders - As many as desired (any age)

Casting and Cutting Note:
Many roles may be doubled if desired. This show was
written to accommodate a cast of 12-20. If you are
performing with a smaller number of actors, cutting scenes
or characters is permitted, and perhaps even admirable. For
changes other than cuts, approval from Uproar Theatrics is
required.

Scene 1

(The Castle. Two bored looking guards stand guard. Enter FRED, excited. He is nervous.)

FRED

(To the audience.) The prince is coming! *(Pause.)* Oh no, you're going to get me in trouble. You have to *stand* when the prince comes in or I will never hear the end of it. So when I say "the prince is coming," *please* stand up.

GUARD 1(MILDRED)

We're already standing. *(Fred startles.)*

FRED

Don't *do* that. My nerves.

GUARD 1 (MILDRED)

I just pointed out that we're already standing.

GUARD 2

Mildred. Don't mind her. She's new.

(MILDRED approaches FRED and extends her hand.)

MILDRED

Hi, I'm Mildred. I'm new.

(FRED uncomfortably shakes her hand.)

FRED

I'm Fred. The Prince's chief servant.

MILDRED

Great, great. I bet that's a sweet gig. How'd you land that?

FRED

I drew the short straw.

(Pause.)

GUARD 2

I'm sorry about her. *Mildred.* Get back to your post. He's trying to talk to *them. (Indicates the audience.)*

MILDRED

Oh, wow, when did they get here? Hi, folks! I'm Mildred, and I'm new!

FRED

Okay, I need to talk to them now. And I highly recommend you return to your spot before the Prince comes in. He has high expectations.

MILDRED

Oooh, okay. Now's my chance to impress middle management. Got it.

(She returns to her post.)

FRED

As I was saying, remember to stand when I announce the Prince. And when he comes in, clap as loud as you can or else he'll think you don't like him anymore. Now...THE PRINCE IS COMING! *(hopefully the audience will stand.)* Remember to clap when he comes in!

(Trumpet's sound. TAD *enters with* SYLVIA. *If the audience does not clap,* FRED *will remind them by clapping. Actors can also be planted in the audience as* AUDIENCE LEADERS *to help lead the applause and later interactions.* TAD

soaks up the applause for a moment before
waving the audience quiet.)

TAD

Greetings, my subjects. *(Pause. Some audience members
might say "greetings," or "hello." TAD looks at FRED in
an accusatory manner.)* You didn't tell them.

FRED

I did, sire! I told them to stand—

TAD

Yes.

FRED

And I told them to clap.

TAD

Yes.

FRED

Yes.

TAD

And...?

FRED

And? Oh! I forgot! Good people:

TAD

Subjects.

FRED

Subjects: when the prince says "greetings my subjects," you
are supposed to reply, "greetings my handsome and
magnanimous lord."

TAD

Thank you. Greetings, my subjects!

FRED and AUDIENCE LEADERS

(Leading the crowd.) Greetings my handsome and magnanimous lord.

TAD

Greetings my subjects!

FRED and AUDIENCE LEADERS

Greetings my handsome and magnanimous lord!

TAD

Thank you. You may sit.

(FRED sits.)

TAD

Not you! Up.

FRED

Sorry sire.

TAD

You are an idiot.

FRED

Thank you, sire.

TAD

My people! I have brought you here today to announce a fantastical bit of news: I am engaged to be married.

(FRED gets the audience to clap.)

4

AUDIENCE LEADER(s)
Woohoo! Yes, Tad! You're the best! Etc.

TAD
Thank you, thank you. Her name is Sylvia, but to you, she shall be called "most beautiful and mild princess."

> *(A few protesters appear in the audience, perhaps holding signs citing their complaints, such as "clean up the horse poop," "privatize executions," or "blood-letting is a right, not a privilege.")*

PROTESTOR 1
What do we want?

OTHER PROTESTORS
A better kingdom.

PROTESTOR 1
When do we want it?

OTHER PROTESTORS
Whenever the king can get to it!

TAD
What is this insolence?

PROTESTOR 4
What do we want?

OTHER PROTESTORS
A better kingdom!

PROTESTOR 4
When do we want it?

OTHER PROTESTORS
Whenever the king can get to it!

TAD
How *dare* you interrupt this show of patriotic support?

PROTESTOR 2
Prince Tad, we demand an audience with the king!

PROTESTOR 3
Yeah, audience with the king!

PROTESTOR 2
We demand to talk to him now!

PROTESTOR 3
Yeah, talk to him now!

PROTESTOR 2
Hey, stop copying me.

PROTESTOR 3
Yeah, stop copying--oh, right. Sorry.

PROTESTOR 1
If you don't summon him now, we'll--

TAD
--you'll what?

PROTESTOR 1
we'll...keep protesting?

PROTESTOR 3
Yeah, we'll keep protesting!

TAD

Guards, see them out!

MILDRED

Yes, some action! Let's go!

GUARD 2

Mildred, remember your training--calm, focused, efficient.

MILDRED

Right! *(Calmly.)* Come with us, and you will be treated fairly.

PROTESTOR 4

Ha! I'll believe it when I see it.

PROTESTOR 3

Yeah, believe it when I see it!

(The guards calmly take hold of the protesters and start to lead them out.)

TAD

Take them to a cell while they await judgment. Away, you rapscallions!

(The protestors get led away, chanting as they go.)

PROTESTORS

Tad is bad! Tad is bad! Tad is bad!

AUDIENCE LEADER(s)

Tad is good! Yay, Tad! We love him! Etc.

(The protestors and guards exit.)

TAD

Subjects, I am sorry you had to see such an ungrateful show of ingratitude. I know you all know that this is the greatest kingdom in the history of kingdoms, and that I, your favorite, am a major part of that. Fred, please lead them in *the cheer.*

FRED

Right! Everyone, repeat after me: "we're the best!" *(Audience repeats.)* "Yaaaaay us!" *(Audience repeats.)* "Hooray for Tad!" *(Audience repeats.)*

> *(*FRED *repeats the cheer with the audience a couple of times, and as he does so, the* GUARDS *return to their posts.)*

TAD

Now that we have that ugliness behind us, I can finish what I know you all want to hear: my complete engagement announcement. Subjects, Sylvia and shall celebrate our nuptials on--

> *(*ERNEST *bursts on stage. This startles* FRED.*)*

ERNEST

--Tad! Sorry to interrupt. Pops need to talk to you right now.

TAD

I'm sure you meant "handsome prince: father, the king, must converse with you."

ERNEST

Sure.

TAD

Well I couldn't possibly come right now. I am addressing my subjects.

ERNEST

I'm sure the people will understand if *the King* needs to speak with you.

(Pause.)

TAD

Sometimes I hate you.

(Pause.)

ERNEST

So I'll tell him you're coming.

(ERNEST exits.)

TAD

Fred. Extend my apologies. Sylvia!

*(*TAD *exits with* SYLVIA *in tow.* FRED *looks at the audience.)*

FRED

I'm—I'm sorry.

*(*FRED *turns to exit.)*

MILDRED

How did I do?

*(*FRED *gives her a "thumbs up" and exits.)*

MILDRED

Yes! I smell a promotion.

(Blackout.)

Scene 2

*(The royal judging and meeting room. KING sits
in his meeting chair. He is quite old and weak,
but has an overbearing presence. An ELDERLY
GUARD stands in the corner. A PEASANT
stands before the KING.)*

PEASANT

You see, my liege, I was framed by my brother's girlfriend's
nephew's aunt. *She* stole the bread and cleverly hid it in my
hand and mouth.

KING

(To the elderly guard.) Phil, what do you think about this?
(No response; he is asleep.) Phil?

PEASANT

Not much of a guard, is he?

KING

Silence, peasant! Phil has provided me excellent service for
decades. *PHIL!*

(PHIL startles awake.)

PHIL

My king, look out! An assassin! Don't worry, I'll get him.

*(PHIL threateningly shuffles toward
PEASANT.)*

KING

No need. He's not an assassin, merely a thief.

PHIL

A thief! Don't worry, I'll get him!

KING

Phil. Stop. I just need you to bring him to the sentencing enforcement office. Peasant, you are sentenced to three years labor on the mud farm.

PEASANT

For stealing a loaf of bread?

KING

It was a whole loaf? My apologies. Four years!

PEASANT

We'll see about that. Can't catch me, Phil!

(PEASANT *runs out of the room.*)

PHIL

Don't worry, I'll get him!

(PHIL *slowly shuffles out of the room, passing*
TAD *and* ERNEST *as they enter.*)

ERNEST

Go get 'em, Phil!

PHIL

I shall!

(PHIL exits.)

KING

Hello, my sons.

ERNEST

Dad, I think it might be time for Phil to retire.

TAD

Don't be absurd. Phil has faithfully served our father for seven decades. Would you throw that hero to the streets?

ERNEST

Well no, but--

KING

Sons.

TAD

Dearest sire.

KING

Please sit. I must speak with you.

(They sit.)

TAD

Yes, dear father?

ERNEST

What's up, dad?

KING

My sons. More than 50 years ago, I became king.

TAD

And an excellent king, my liege.

KING

At the time, I was only in my 40s, and I had a lot of learning to do. But I knew one thing: as king, my main job was to make sure that the kingdom would always be...exactly the same as it always has been.

TAD

And you have done a wonderful job.

KING

But I will not be around forever. Soon, I will leave this earth, and you, Tad, will become King.

TAD

Thank you, father.

KING

Unless you die, run away, or unexpectedly disappear. In that case, Ernest, you will be Tad's successor.

ERNEST

I mean, I kind of figured that, but thanks, dad.

TAD

Father, I don't mean to question your judgment or anything, but...shouldn't my wife or maybe my child become my successor?

KING

NO! This is as it always has been, therefore it is right. You may go.

TAD

Can we just talk about--

KING

Go. I will see you at dinner.

> *(TAD and ERNEST look at each other and exit
> quietly. As they leave, the guards lead in the
> PROTESTORS.)*

KING

Three at once. What is the crime?

MILDRED

Expressing a desire for change, sire.

KING

Diabolical...

> *(The lights fade.)*

Scene 3

> *(The royal forest. Enter TAD and FRED. With
> sack lunches.)*

TAD

That useless twit. "Dad needs to talk to you right now."
Couldn't he see I was busy? Probably just jealous that the
people don't like *him*. They wouldn't *care* if he got married,
they wouldn't even care if he *died*.

FRED

What did the King need you for?

TAD

So stupid! All he needed was to tell me "I'm not gonna be around forever, and when I die, you get the kingdom." Well *duh*! But you know what he said?—

FRED

No.

TAD

--He said that if *I* died, that Ernest was gonna take over. *Ernest!* That useless twit!

FRED

What's wrong with Ernest?

TAD

He has no respect for traditions! He would change everything! Also, he's just, you know, not as good as me.

FRED

Well who else would it be?

TAD

I dunno, someone of *my* choosing, maybe, oh I don't know, my new *princess*. Don't you think that someone of my choosing would have more of a right to rule the kingdom than some useless twit who happens to be the King's son?

FRED

Of course, my prince.

TAD

You hungry? I'm hungry.

FRED

Not rea—

TAD

Let's have some lunch.

(They sit and open their sack lunches.)

TAD

Oh, man! Who packs these things?

FRED

Your helpers.

TAD

They're not *helpers* Fred, they're called *servants*. If they
want to be called "helpers," then they should do something
helpful for once and pack me a *good* lunch, not this,
this...*stupid* lunch.

FRED

What's wrong with peanut butter and jelly?

TAD

It's *boring*, that's what. And what's with the apple? Every
time I open a sack lunch, there's an apple in it. I don't like
apples! *(Pause.)* What have you got?

FRED

Nothing special.

(TAD grabs the bag and looks in.)

TAD

What?! A burger, chips, a Twinkie, and a soda? Who
packed this?

FRED

I did.

(Pause.)

TAD

Wanna trade me anything? I've got this amazing apple.
Look how shiny and red it is.

FRED

I'll stick with what I have.

> *(TAD watches FRED eat his Twinkie for a
> moment, and then grudgingly starts eating his
> sandwich. WITCH enters, dressed shabbily.)*

TAD

Hey Fred.

FRED

What.

TAD

Here comes a winner.

FRED

How so, sire?

TAD

Well. Uh. I bet she wins the worst-dressed contest *every*
year.

> *(WITCH walks closer to the two men. FRED
> smiles at her, and she nods in return. TAD tries
> not to notice her.)*

WITCH

How's your lunch?

                    FRED
Great. You hungry?

                    WITCH
I am.

                    FRED
Want my chips?

                    WITCH
How's *your* lunch?

          (Pause.)

                    FRED
Sire.

                    TAD
What? Oh. Hello.

                    WITCH
How's your lunch?

                    TAD
It's okay. Thank you. Have a nice day.

                    WITCH
I do love apples.

                    TAD
That's great. Run along.

                    WITCH
Are you eating your apple?

                    TAD
No, I'm eating my sandwich.

18

WITCH

I'd like to have your apple, if I may.

TAD

You may *not*.

WITCH

You will give me that apple.

TAD

Aha, miss. I don't think you understand the notion of
property. This apple is mine. Therefore, it is up to me to
decide who I give it to.

WITCH

And you will give it to me.

TAD

Miss! You're bothering me. Go away.

WITCH

Give me your apple, or you will suffer the consequences.

TAD

And what might those be? You'll stay here and I'll have to
smell you for the rest of my lunch?

WITCH

You have one more chance. Give me that apple, or you will
suffer the consequences.

TAD

Smelly woman! You're weirding me out! Do you know who
I am? I am the Prince, and you cannot order a Prince
around, especially if you're poor, smelly, and ugly. You must
leave now, or *you* will suffer the consequences. You have ten
seconds to start on your merry way—

WITCH

Tad, son of the King, brother of Ernest, and fiance of Sylvia,
I condemn you to a life of minutia and irony.

> *(She brandishes a wand, points it at him, and
> yells, "Frog!" TAD shrinks to the ground, now
> nothing more than a frog.)*

WITCH

In this form you will remain until the day you discover what
it is to love someone other than yourself and receive a kiss of
love in return. I do not think such a day will come.

> *(WITCH exits.)*

TAD

Ribbit.

> *(FRED walks away. TAD follows.)*

Scene 4

> *(ERNEST and SYLVIA enter. They are
> searching for TAD.)*

ERNEST

Tad!

                           SYLVIA

Tad?

                           ERNEST

Tad!

                           SYLVIA

Tad?

                           ERNEST

TAD!!!

                           SYLVIA
It's no use, we'll never find him this way.

                           ERNEST

What do you suggest?

                           SYLVIA
(She calls.) Handsome and magnanimous lord!

                           ERNEST

Oh mighty Prince!

                           SYLVIA

Let's go this way.

                    (They exit as TAD *and* FRED *enter in another
                    part of the forest.)*

                            TAD
I gotta tell ya Fred. I just can't cover as much ground as a
frog.

                            FRED

I noticed.

TAD

What took us one morning to walk when I was human has
already taken us two days to re-trace.

FRED

Yes.

TAD

It's a good thing I like flies now, otherwise I'd be really
hungry.

FRED

Yes.

TAD

And it's a good thing you like berries so much, 'cause
you've had plenty of *those* to eat.

FRED

I *don't* like berries.

TAD

You don't? Then why have you been eating so *many*?

FRED

It's that or leaves.

TAD

Well, don't you worry. We should be back to the castle in *no*
time. Bet they're wondering where I am. Ribbit.

FRED

Mm.

TAD

You think they'll *recognize* me? I mean. I know I'm a frog,
but. Don't I at least bear *some* resemblance to my former
self?

FRED

No sire.

TAD

Drat! Do I at least *sound* the same?

FRED

Similar sire.

TAD

Yes. Yes, that should be enough.

(TAD tries to hop, but he falls on his face.)

TAD

Yup. Still not used to hopping.

(ERNEST and SYLVIA enter.)

SYLVIA

Fred!

ERNEST

Fred!

FRED

Hello.

TAD

Ernest! Sylvia!

(Pause.)

ERNEST

Where's the prince?

TAD

I'm right here, you idiot.

SYLVIA

Fred?

FRED

Mm?

SYLVIA

Where's Tad?

TAD

I'm here, I said, I'm *right here.*

FRED

He's...

(FRED *gestures toward the frog-ified* TAD.)

ERNEST

Where?

FRED

Right there.

ERNEST

What, the *frog?*

(FRED *nods. Pause.* ERNEST *laughs.*)

ERNEST

Yeah, I get it, he can be kinda frog-like sometimes, but really. Where'd he go? We haven't seen him for two days.

TAD

What?! *Frog*-like? How *dare* you.

FRED

They don't seem to hear you.

SYLVIA

Fred. We think the frog joke was cute, but we really want to find him. We have some bad news. The king is dead. Did Tad know that? Is that why he ran away?

TAD

I didn't run away, that wouldn't make any *sense.* I was simply turned into a *frog,* that's all.

FRED

I don't know where he is.

TAD

What?!

FRED

Sorry.

ERNEST

That's okay, we'll keep looking. If you see him, tell him to go home at once.

FRED

He may be back there already.

ERNEST

Right. Well, let's go. Be careful not to step on the frog.

SYLVIA

Bye, Fred.

(ERNEST and SYLVIA exit.)

TAD

That doesn't make any sense.

FRED

What?

TAD

Why would they just ignore me like that?

FRED

I don't think they were ignoring you, I think they couldn't *hear* you.

TAD

Now *that* doesn't make any sense either. How can *you* hear me if *they* can't?

FRED

Maybe it's a plot device.

TAD

Or maybe, only those who are pure in heart can hear me. You know, like in those fairy tales. Ribbit.

FRED

But then you wouldn't be able to hear *yourself*.

TAD

Hey, watch it.

FRED

What?

TAD

You can't talk to me like that, I'm your *prince*.

FRED

You're a frog. And by the looks of it, Ernest is set to be King.

TAD

Aah! You're *right*. This calls for drastic action!

FRED

Such as?

(Pause.)

TAD

I don't know.

FRED

Brilliant. Well, in the meantime, I'm going to figure out how to start up a fire, and perhaps make up some rudimentary spears to hunt some small critters so I can eat something *significant* tonight.

TAD

Aren't we going to keep heading for the castle?

FRED

What's the point? Ernest and Sylvia can't hear you and would never believe me that you are the Prince. And now they think I'm crazy, so odds are I'm out of a job. So now, I'm fending for myself. Tag along if you want.

*(*FRED *exits,* TAD *follows.)*

TAD

Wait! Slow down! I'm a frog!

(He falls down and exits.)

Scene 5

(A different part of the royal forest. There is a hut. PEASANT runs on, pauses and looks behind him.)

PEASANT

You still back there, Phil? Can't catch me! Ha ha, ha ha ha!

(PEASANT runs off stage, crossing paths with FRED who enters, walking with purpose. PHIL enters, winded.)

FRED

Oh, hi, Phil.

PHIL

My liege, is that you?

FRED

No, it's Fred, Tad's servant.

PHIL

Ah, yes, sonny.

FRED

The peasant you're chasing went that way.

(FRED points offstage in the direction of PEASANT. PHIL hobbles out in that direction.)

PHIL

Don't worry, I'll get him.

(PHIL *exits.* TAD *hollers off-stage.*)

TAD (offstage)

Fred! Where are you?

FRED

Right here.

TAD (offstage)

Where?

FRED

Right here. Umm...in the woods? Does that help?

TAD (offstage)

Of course not!

FRED

Follow my voice, then.

(*Silence.*)

TAD (offstage)

I can't follow your voice if you stop talking!

FRED

What would you like me to say?

(TAD *enters, out of breath.*)

TAD

Finally, there you are. Yeesh. Give me a second to breathe.
Woooo boy. Oooof.

FRED

Are you okay.

TAD

Yeahhhhhh. Huuuuuuuh. I'm good. Where are you leading us, anyway?

FRED

Right here. *(He gestures to the hut.)*

TAD

Woah woah woah wait. Are we still in the Royal Wood?

FRED

Yes.

TAD

This hut is in violation of the Royal Wood Anti-Inhabitation Act.

FRED

What are you doing to go about it?

TAD

I mean nothing right now. Step one is don't be a frog anymore. But once that happens, I will be contacting the *rangers*.

FRED

Well, I'm hoping the one who lives in this hut can heal you. So maybe relax a bit.

TAD

Oh, I see. I will reserve judgment.

FRED

Great. I'm going to knock. You just hang back.

(FRED *approaches the hut and knocks on the door.*)

HEALER (offstage)

Nobody home.

(FRED *looks at* TAD *who shrugs.*)

TAD

Try again. Maybe nobody heard you.

FRED

*Some*body heard me, they just said "nobody home."

TAD

Right. Good thinking. Clever.

(FRED *knocks again.*)

FRED

We know you're home, just open the door.

HEALER (offstage)

We have a permit to be here, go away.

FRED

We're not rangers, we're here for a healing.

(HEALER *steps out.*)

HEALER

Who sent you? How do you know about me? What kind of healing?

FRED

Uh, I sent me. You brought my father back from the dead ten years ago, and--

HEALER

--I brought...yes, yes, I *did* do that once. That was a heck of a thing. Wow, it's been a while. *Ten* years? Time, am I right? You must be Frederick Marzipan Jr, then.

FRED

Yes, that's--

TAD

--wait, what? That's your name?

HEALER

Who's the frog?

TAD

Excuse me, you woodland peasant. Do not condescend to your prince.

> (*A pause. Then* HEALER *begins to laugh.* FRED *follows.* TAD *doesn't laugh.*)

HEALER

Hey, Marge, come check this guy out!

> (*They continue to laugh, and* TAD *gets increasingly upset.* MARGE *enters from the hut.*)

MARGE

What do you want, I'm in the middle of bottling the snake oil.

HEALER

This talking frog says he's a prince!

TAD

I *am* the prince!

(They laugh all the harder.)

TAD

What is this insolence! Fred, put an end to this at once!

(They're still laughing.)

FRED

Alright, alright. Yes, yes, it's very funny, but that's enough.
This is Prince Tad. And he has gotten himself into this, uh,
predicament, and we're hoping you might be able to restore
him to his human self?

HEALER

What do you think, Marge?

MARGE

We've never done a frog transformation before. If he was at
least a *mammal*...

HEALER

I know, but...this is *Frederick Marzipan Jr.*

MARGE

Oh, go on.

HEALER

No, really.

FRED

Hi.

HEALER

Don't you remember, Marge? The glory days. We had the
best business of our lives after we resurrected his father.
And if word gets around that we could turn this *frog* back
into prince *Tad*...we could double our rates.

MARGE

I don't know...

HEALER

You could afford to see a doctor about your bunions.

MARGE

...seems risky. What if we accidentally kill him? He's the
prince. That would be bad.

FRED

Nobody would know but us.

TAD

Hey, I'm right here.

MARGE

Alright. Let's try it.

HEALER

But first, we need to know how it happened.

FRED

Well, you see, Tad was--

TAD

--it was this smelly witch woman! She was all, "give me
your apple," and I was all, "no, I like my apple," and then
BLAM! I'm a frog.

HEALER

This witch...did she give you a way to break the spell?

TAD

It has something to do with love and kissing.

> (HEALER *and* MARGE *cry out and begin to do some kind of ritual in reaction to this news. It can involve things like turning, chanting, spinning, stomping, or whatever. They finally stop.)*

MARGE

We dare not help you!

HEALER

Sorry, Frederick. We know this witch. She pervades these woods. Nobody will help you.

FRED

But--

> (HEALER *and* MARGE *exit, leaving* FRED *and* TAD *alone in the woods once again.)*

TAD

Well *that's* not good.

> *(Blackout.)*

Scene 6

> *(Enter* HELEN, *a peasant. She speaks to the audience.)*

HELEN

I'm so distraught!

(She exits as TAD *and* FRED *enter.* FRED *is carrying rudimentary spears.)*

TAD

You've become quite the hunter in only a few months. At least...I *think* it's been a few months since we were gone...is that right?

FRED

I haven't been counting.

TAD

Well we should start. We could put little marks on one of your spears for each day. And after a year passes, we should have a party. Like a birthday party, but really it's more like a death day party. Or perhaps a...uh...*frog* day party. That's it!

FRED

But it won't be accurate.

TAD

Who cares! It's an excuse to party!

FRED

Who are we gonna party with, *Tad,* other frogs?

(Pause.)

TAD

I don't think I'm quite adjusted to you calling me "Tad."

FRED

It's your *name*.

TAD

But I am the *prince.* I may be a frog, but I'm not *dead.* That witch didn't *kill* me. *(Pause.)* Could you at least call me "*prince* Tad?"

FRED

I—

TAD

It just occurred to me!

FRED

What?

TAD

The witch!

FRED

Yes?

TAD

Her curse, do you remember her curse?

FRED

Something about you being selfish and needing to learn to love someone else. Something.

TAD

The other part! She cursed me to a life of, what, minutia and irony? Right?

FRED

K.

TAD

I just got the irony part! My name is Tad*!*

FRED

What, like small?

TAD

And like *tadpole!*

FRED

Huh. That's pretty good.

TAD

Suddenly I have more appreciation for my situation.

> (TAD *starts to laugh hard. He laughs until he*
> *begins to cry. He sobs.)*

FRED

What is it?

TAD

I'm a *frog!* Named *Tad!* Look at me! I was once heir to the
kingdom!

FRED

At least your life has been interesting.

TAD

Who cares?! I'm so upset! I'm—

> (HELEN *suddenly enters, sobbing, and*
> *collapses at the other side of the stage.* TAD
> *and* FRED *freeze.)*

TAD

Fred, what is that?

FRED

A young peasant woman, I think.

                                TAD

Roughly my age?

                    (FRED *glances her way. She has not noticed
                    them.)*

                                FRED

In human years, yes.

                                TAD

Blonde? Brunette? Redhead?

                                FRED

Why does it matter?

                                TAD

I want to know if she's my type.

                                FRED

Amphibious is your type.

                                TAD

Think you could introduce me?

                                FRED

Do it yourself.

                    (He turns TAD *around and pushes him toward*
                    HELEN.)

                                TAD
(Clears his throat.) Good day, miss.

                    (She does not look up.)

HELEN

Hi.

(She continues to cry. TAD doesn't know what to do. He looks to FRED for help.)

FRED

...what's wrong...

TAD

What's the matter, you look terrible.

(She cries all the louder.)

FRED

What'd you say that for?

TAD

I've never been good with women.

FRED

What about Sylvia?

TAD

When you're a prince you don't *have* to be good with women.

FRED

You're gonna have to say *something*, you've upset her.

TAD

Like what?

FRED

I don't know, cheer her up.

TAD

Okay. Cheer her up. Right. *(He turns to her,)* Knock knock.

HELEN

...who's there...

TAD

Interrupting frog.

HELEN

...interrupting frog—

TAD

Ribbit!

(Pause. She begins to laugh.)

HELEN

That's funny. Thank you for— *(She turns, looks up, and notices him.)* AAAAAAHHHHH!!!!!!

TAD

AAAH!

HELEN

You're a frog! What's the matter with me?! I'm talking to a frog!!!

(Pause.)

TAD

It's true. I am a frog.

FRED

But he's not just any frog.

                            TAD
It's true. I'm actually—

                            FRED
He's a *talking* frog.

                            TAD
Let's just say there's more to me than meets the eye.

                            HELEN
I see.

                            TAD
I'm Tad.

                            HELEN
(After a chuckle.) That's pretty funny.

                            TAD
Yes, well. What were you upset about a minute ago?

                            HELEN
Oh. I don't want to talk about it.

            (TAD looks to FRED for help, who shrugs.)

                            TAD
Well...if ever you *do* want to talk about it...I'd be happy to
listen?

                    *(He checks with FRED, who gives him a thumbs
                    up sign.)*

                            HELEN
Thank you, but I think I need some more time. I'm gonna
go. Thanks for cheering me up a little.

(She exits.)

TAD

I like her.

FRED

You're engaged, Tad.

TAD

I haven't seen her in months! She's certainly moved on by now.

FRED

Still.

TAD

I know, I know. It would be wrong of me to—

(HELEN suddenly enters.)

HELEN

I was crying because my husband died and left me with nothing and because of the patriarchal societal construct I have not been given any chance to learn a trade thereby making me useless to society so I ran away in hopes of finding a society that would give me the chance to be more than an object to be patronized.

TAD

Those are big words.

HELEN

I'm lost in the woods and you're the first people I've seen in at least a week and you're a frog!

TAD

But I'm also a person.

HELEN

But you can see why I'm distraught.

TAD

Yes. I'm sorry for the loss of your husband. And I'm sorry I'm a frog.

HELEN

He was a jerk anyway.

TAD

Then you're upset because...

HELEN

I have been forced to the fringes by the patriarchal societal construct.

TAD

Of course. And this...parrotizing social conflict...it can't be...worked out?

(HELEN laughs.)

HELEN

You're cute.

TAD

Thank you.

HELEN

In a little froggy sort of way. Of course you couldn't understand the way of things as a frog.

TAD

Well then...maybe you could tell me about the way of things?

HELEN

It's very simple. The kingdom is run by *men,* and until very recently, was run by a very *old* man, whose ways were bordering on tyrannical.

TAD

Tyranny-what?

HELEN

It means he was an evil ruler!

TAD

What?! I'll have you know that the king was not *evil*—

HELEN

What do you know about it? You're a frog.

TAD

Yes, we're agreed on that fact.

HELEN

And his son was no better.

TAD

What?!

HELEN

I know. It's hard to imagine.

TAD

(Through clenched teeth.) Go on.

HELEN

In my village, it is the law that men get to do all the learning and the working and we women just get to sit around looking pretty.

TAD

Well you *are* very pretty.

HELEN

That's not the point! I had to marry the first decent-enough man who offered—I couldn't make it on my own. And then he up and *died* and didn't leave me a penny. You know why?

TAD

Why?

HELEN

It is written that when a man dies, the *king* gets all of his wealth! Can you believe that?

TAD

Well, there's all the roads to upkeep, and, you know, the uh, palace staff, and everything.

HELEN

And you want to know the best part?

TAD

What?

HELEN

The day after they took everything, the new king did away with that stupid law.

TAD

The new king?

HELEN

King Ernest. The old king's second son. He knew the law was stupid, so he removed it from the books. Didn't help *me* any.

TAD

So. *Ernest* is king now.

HELEN

Yes. And the kingdom is better for it. He sees that he can make changes that would make life better for the little peasant folk like us. And now that he's got Queen Sylvia by his side—

TAD

He married Sylvia!

HELEN

--they can only be a force for good in this kingdom. But I'm not going to wait around for everything to get better. There have got to be places out there that are better right now. I just can't find my way out of these woods.

TAD

Well...you could travel with *us* if you want. I don't know if it'll help you find your way out, but at least we have rudimentary spears to hunt things.

HELEN

I don't know.

TAD

Fred here could teach you to hunt and build fires, that sort of thing.

HELEN

Could you?

FRED

Sure. But we have no desire to *leave* the forest, so...

HELEN

That's fine. It's better than wandering aimlessly by myself.

TAD

Great. Our camp is this way.` *(They exit.)*

Scene 7

(Enter ERNEST *and* SYLVIA. *At the palace.)*

SYLVIA

It's been three months. I think it's time we had a funeral.

ERNEST

We still don't know he's dead. He could be...I dunno...hiding in the woods somewhere.

SYLVIA

Yes. And we searched the woods for days only to find his servant spouting some nonsense about him being a frog.

ERNEST

Yeah.

SYLVIA

If you want my opinion, Fred killed him.

ERNEST

What?!

SYLVIA

Think about it. Tad finds out the king is dead, so he runs away to the forest for a few hours to "find himself." Fred, who's been treated badly by Tad for years, takes opportunity into his hands and kills him. Perhaps with some rudimentary

SYLVIA (cont)

spear made out of a stick. We find him a couple days later and, in a panic, he spouts off some nonsense about a frog.

ERNEST

Huh. You may be on to something. But what if you're wrong and he comes back? He's the rightful heir. The kingdom would be his.

SYLVIA

Come on. Do you *really* think Tad would delay his opportunity to be king? He's not coming back.

ERNEST

Yeah, you're right.

SILVIA

Besides, a funeral would be good for the kingdom. They could finally put Tad behind them.

ERNEST

Yes.

SYLVIA

I could put Tad behind *me*.

ERNEST

Yeah. But let me just check with one more person. Head guard, Mildred!

(MILDRED *enters, confidently, with* GUARD 2 *behind, hanging back.*)

MILDRED

Sire.

ERNEST

Report on the latest search efforts for Tad. Please.

MILDRED

Certainly. We've searched the forest, the moat, the dungeon,
the towers, the closets, the outhouse, the dragon's lair, and
the diner.

ERNEST

The dragon's lair? Wow.

MILDRED

Had to slay that thing myself. Yeah, I'm pretty great.

ERNEST

I'll say. What about the surrounding kingdoms?

MILDRED

Underling! Any updates from the surrounding kingdoms
lately?

GUARD 2

Nobody's seen him. Even Rapunzel, and she sees everything
from up there.

ERNEST

Alright. Thank you. A funeral it is. Let's go talk to the party
planner.

> (ERNEST *and* SYLVIA *exit. As soon as they
> are gone,* MILDRED *let's her "guard" down.)*

MILDRED

Gol-ly being head guard is a heck of a thing.

> *(She lies face down on the floor.)*

MILDRED

You claw your way to the top, and what's there, you know?

GUARD 2

I don't.

MILDRED

Nothing but higher expectations!

GUARD 2

And a higher paycheck.

MILDRED

I mean, my worklife-homelife balance is just shot.

GUARD 2

There there.

(Blackout.)

Scene 8

*(The River. HELEN enters, awkwardly carrying
a rudimentary spear. She rears back as if to
throw it, but drops it behind her. As she picks it
up, FRED enters.)*

FRED

Still having trouble holding onto it?

HELEN

Yes.

FRED

You're still afraid of it. Remember: it's an extension of
yourself.

HELEN

Yeah, you keep *telling* me that.

(FRED *stands behind her and positions the
spear in her hand, over her shoulder.)*

FRED

And *you* just need to *believe* it.

(She is speechless for a moment as his hand
touches hers.)

HELEN

...so, you uh...think I could eventually get good at this?

(TAD *enters with a handful of bugs.* FRED *still
has his hand on* HELEN's.)

FRED

Just become one with the spear.

TAD

Sorry to interrupt. You going fishing soon? I caught you
some *flies.*

FRED

...that's great, Tad.

HELEN

Thanks! I was just thinking fish would be good for dinner.

TAD

Glad I could be of some service.

HELEN

Yeah, fishing would be fun. More spear training tomorrow, Fred?

FRED

Yes ma'am.

TAD

Ribbit.

HELEN

Let's fish, then!

TAD

Yeah, but I should leave before you do. It was really hard to catch them and not eat them...if I see you throw one in the water, I might jump in after it.

FRED

So?

TAD

I can't swim. And a big fish might eat me.

HELEN

That's okay. We'll wait.

TAD

Thanks—OH THERE'S A FLY OVER THERE!

> *(He jumps after a fly, but it's in the water. He tries to stop himself, but he falls in.)*

HELEN

Oh no, he fell in!

                    TAD

Help!

          (Any number of fish spot him and swim towards
          TAD to eat him.)

                    FISH

Frog frog frog.

                    TAD

FISH! FISH! *FIIIIIIISH!*

                    FISH

FROG FROG *FROOOOOOOG!*

                    HELEN

Hold on! I'll get you!

          (A brief chase ensues as she jumps in, catches
          up to him, scares off the fish, and pulls TAD to
          shore. TAD is shrieking.)

                    TAD

FISH! FISH! FISH!

                    HELEN

It's okay.

                    TAD

MOMMY!!!

                    HELEN

You're okay. It's okay. Shh...

                    TAD

I'm okay. I'm okay.

FRED

You alright?

TAD

Yeah. Yeah. Phew. Helen. You saved me.

HELEN

That's what you do when you care about someone.

TAD

You care about me?

HELEN

I do.

TAD

That's *great.*

> *(He's about to try to kiss her, but he realizes*
> FRED *is there, so he stops.)*

TAD

I like you too. I'm gonna go so you can fish.

> *(He exits awkwardly.)*

FRED

That was interesting.

HELEN

I hope he's okay.

FRED

Let's go further downriver where the deep part is.

HELEN

Good idea.

(They exit.)

Scene 9

(RABBIT enters as if being chased. It stops and looks around.)

RABBIT

Oh, good, I think I lost them. Never a dull moment when you're at the bottom of the food chain.

(HELEN runs on, carrying a rudimentary spear. She looks around for something.)

RABBIT

OH MY LETTUCE AND CARROTS!

(RABBIT hides somewhere on stage.)

HELEN

Nuts.

(FRED runs on shortly after her with another spear.)

FRED

Where'd it go?

HELEN

Lost it.

FRED

Nuts.

HELEN

I know.

FRED

That's okay. We have plenty to eat tonight. You're getting quite good with that spear.

HELEN

I owe it all to you.

>*(They look into each other's eyes for a moment.*
>TAD *soon enters, winded.)*

TAD

Wait up, guys, geez. I can't run like you can.

HELEN

We just think it's funny to watch you try.

TAD

Oh ha ha ha. Jerks.

FRED

You caught up with us just fine, it just took you a minute.

TAD

Well. I'm gonna sit here and rest for a bit. You can run along and do your little hunting thing if you want, but I'm gonna sit.

FRED

Works for me. Helen?

HELEN

You go ahead and try to find that rabbit. I'm going to sit with Tad for a bit.

FRED

Suit yourself. I'll catch up with you guys later.

> *(FRED runs off in the opposite direction of where RABBIT was hiding. RABBIT starts to tiptoe offstage as TAD and HELEN sit quietly for a moment. TAD notices the rabbit.)*

TAD

Hey!

HELEN

What?

> *(RABBIT silently pleads to TAD to be quiet. TAD decides to let RABBIT get away.)*

TAD

Nothing.

HELEN

Okay. *(Awkward silence.)* Hey, Tad?

TAD

Hmm?

HELEN

I've, uh. I've never thanked you. For letting me join you guys.

TAD

No?

HELEN

No. And I want you to know...that I'm really glad I did.

TAD

So am I. You're a wonderful woman.

HELEN

You've changed my life. I can't imagine where I would be
right now if I hadn't run into you.

TAD

There's something I've been wanting to tell you...

HELEN

I never thought.

TAD

I'm not what I appear to be.

HELEN

I never thought I'd ever find love...

TAD

It may surprise you to hear this, but...

HELEN

But because of you, everything has changed.

(The next two lines are together.)

TAD

I'm the prince.

HELEN

I'm in love with Fred.

TAD

Fred?!

HELEN

The Prince?!

HELEN and TAD

I don't believe it! What? Why not?

(The next two lines are also spoken together.)

HELEN

You're a frog!

TAD

You're supposed to love me!

HELEN

Wait a minute: what?

TAD

I'm the one who's supposed to earn your love. Me.

HELEN

What do you mean, *supposed?* And what do you mean
you're the Prince?

TAD

I am Prince Tad. You know. The *evil* one. Just before my
father died, a witch turned me into a frog in this very forest,
and the only thing that can change me back is if I can learn
to love someone other than myself, and earn their love in
return.

HELEN

That's strange.

TAD

Tell me about it.

HELEN

Why me?

TAD

What do you mean?

HELEN

It doesn't *have* to be *me*, does it?

TAD

No, I suppose not. But.

HELEN

But what?

TAD

I felt something back when you told me about your troubles. About how you had no choice but to leave the kingdom. I'd never felt that way before.

HELEN

What did it feel like?

TAD

Like...like the only thing that mattered to me at that moment was making sure you were okay.

HELEN

Maybe that's love.

TAD

It could also have just been sympathy.

HELEN

Still, you cared about someone deeply.

TAD

But the spell isn't broken. I'm still a frog.

(The WITCH *enters, unnoticed by the other characters.)*

HELEN

Yes.

TAD

And you love *Fred*, and. I'm out here in the woods with *very* little chance of meeting someone else. Especially someone as, as...as *pretty*, and. And *smart* as you.

HELEN

Tad. I am *in* love with Fred. But there are other kinds of love. Like friendship.

TAD

Apparently that's not good enough! I'm. still. a. frog.

HELEN

Maybe—

TAD

I can't run like I used to. I can't...I dunno *stand*. Like I used to. I don't have opposable *thumbs*.

HELEN

Yes, but—

TAD

I just...I think I need some time alone.

HELEN

Are you sure?

TAD

Yes. I don't want to be bothering you right now.

HELEN

You're not.

TAD

Yeah but. I just need to think about some things.

HELEN

Okay. Come find me when you want company.

(She kisses him on top of the head and exits.
Music. TAD turns back into a human, but
doesn't notice.)

TAD

Well *that* went well.

(He turns to exit and sees the WITCH. He is
startled by her.)

TAD

Nyuh. Great. What are you gonna do to me *now*?

WITCH

Look.

(Pause. TAD looks around.)

TAD

Am I looking for anything in particular?

WITCH

Look...down.

(He looks down at himself and jumps.)

TAD

Wha?! I'm, I'm *me* again!

(WITCH *turns to exit.*)

TAD

Wait!

WITCH

Hmm?

TAD

May I ask you a question?

WITCH

You want to know why.

TAD

Yes.

WITCH

But don't you already?

TAD

I want to know what I did to deserve getting turned into a frog, losing my kingdom, and losing my fiance to my brother. Not to mention eating all those flies.

WITCH

You liked them at the time.

TAD

That's beside the point.

WITCH

How does it feel to be small?

TAD

Huh?

WITCH

How does it feel. To be small.

TAD

I hate it.

WITCH

Your two friends have spent their whole lives feeling small.

TAD

Yes, but—

WITCH

One as a servant and one as a peasant.

TAD

But at least *they* weren't turned into *frogs.*

WITCH

At least *you* have an opportunity to make the kingdom better for people like *them.*

TAD

I guess I do.

WITCH

You have a kingdom to rule. You are the rightful heir to the throne. Don't let these lessons in size have no effect on you. You can be a great man if you look outside yourself. Find your friends and return to the kingdom. And so I leave you.

> (WITCH *exits. After a moment,* TAD *exits in search of his friends.)*

Scene 10

(ERNEST and SYLVIA enter, looking sad and flanked by the GUARDS. ERNEST addresses the audience.)

ERNEST

People of the kingdom, today we officially mourn the loss of a...an *important* man to this kingdom: Prince Tad. Though he disappeared months ago, we feared, I mean *hoped* that he would return to claim his authority over the land after the death of your dear king, my father. He has not returned. Therefore, good people, we have called you together to acknowledge his presumed death. We could have had a private ceremony, but we know he would have appreciated the attention. *(Pause.)* Princess Sylvia? Anything to add?

SYLVIA

May he rest in peace.

(Pause.)

ERNEST

Anything else?

SYLVIA

That's it.

ERNEST

Okay. Well. Uh, let's send him off right. So on the count of three, let's all say, "goodbye, handsome and magnanimous lord." Got it? Good. One, two, three. *(AUDIENCE LEADERS assist in getting the audience to join in.)* Goodbye, handsome and magnanimous lord.

(TAD enters, followed by HELEN *and* FRED.*)*

TAD

Greetings, my brother!

ERNEST and SYLVIA

Aaah!!!

(They are not looking in TAD's *direction, but
looking around for his ghost.)*

ERNEST

I hear his phantom! Don't punish us, ghost of Tad!

TAD

I'm right here, Ernest.

ERNEST

Aah! You look so real!

*(*TAD *touches* ERNEST *on the shoulder.*
ERNEST *cowers.)*

ERNEST

Don't hurt me!

SYLVIA

I don't think he's dead, Ernest.

ERNEST

Oh. Yes, well.

TAD

Ernest.

ERNEST

(unsure.) Yes...?

(TAD kneels before ERNEST. HELEN and FRED do the same.)

TAD

King Ernest, I give you my allegiance. I am sorry for mistreating you all your life, and I seek your forgiveness.

(ERNEST does not know what to do. He looks to SYLVIA for help. She whispers something in his ear. Suddenly they both kneel to TAD.)

ERNEST

Tad, you are the rightful king of the kingdom. We offer you the kingdom and seek your forgiveness for, uh, changing most of its laws without your consent. And I'm sorry I married your fiance.

(Pause.)

TAD

Well this is rather awkward.

(They each glance up at the other without breaking their kneel/bow. SYLVIA suddenly stands.)

SYLVIA

This is stupid. Stand up. So, who rules the kingdom now?

(Silence.)

FRED

Further awkwardness ensues.

TAD

I propose that we ask the kingdom. It is they who it affects.

SYLVIA

Great, but before we continue. Who's this?

TAD

I'm so sorry. This is Helen. We met her in the forest.

HELEN

Hi.

SYLVIA

Hi.

(She turns to the audience.)

SYLVIA

People of the kingdom! In an exciting turn of events, Prince Tad has returned to us as if from beyond the grave. We need your help in deciding whether he or Ernest shall be the King from this time forward. Will you help us?

(Hopefully the audience will say 'yes.')

AUDIENCE LEADERS

Yeah! You bet we will! Great idea! Etc.

SYLVIA

Great! *(To the other characters, under her breath.)* Now what do we do?

HELEN

How about speeches?

SYLVIA

Great idea! Tad! You're the older. You go first.

(TAD steps forward.)

TAD

Oh, uh. I don't think I should be king. I was a terrible prince
and you all know it. Ernest deserves to be king. He's already
acting as king, and he's doing a great job, and has made
some great changes to help people.

(TAD *steps back.*)

SYLVIA

...okay. Ernest?

(ERNEST *steps up.*)

ERNEST

People of the kingdom. Tad was always meant to be king.
He's the oldest. He's the one the former king named to
follow in his footsteps. I am simply a stand-in. Tad should be
your king.

(ERNEST *steps back.* SYLVIA *looks confused.*)

SYLVIA

...well then. After those...awe inspiring speeches, let's put it
to a vote. All those who think that Tad, the oldest, should
become king, raise your hands. *(A quick count.)* Okay.
Those who think Ernest should simply remain the king, raise
your hands.

> *(What follows will be improvised, depending on
> the outcome. If there is a clear winner, then
> SYLVIA will announce the winner. At which
> time, the winner will thank the audience for
> choosing them and then offer to share the
> responsibility with the loser, who thankfully
> accepts the offer. If the audience is evenly split,
> then SYLVIA announces the tie and declares*

that both will rule the kingdom. After all has
been decided, TAD *speaks to* ERNEST.)

TAD

Ernest. I'm sorry for everything.

ERNEST

I know.

TAD

Will you accept my apology?

ERNEST

I do.

TAD

Thanks.

(PHIL *enters, out of breath and with* PEASANT
in tow.)

PHIL

Sire, I got him.

PEASANT

(To TAD *and* ERNEST) I'm as surprised as you are.

ERNEST

Got who? Who is this?

PHIL

A peasant I have been chasing for...quite some time now...

ERNEST

Well, what did he do?

PHIL

I don't remember...the king just told me to chase him.

ERNEST

Oh, well...

(ERNEST *looks at* TAD, *who shrugs.*)

TAD

Couldn't have been that bad...I dunno...let him go, I guess?

ERNEST

Sure--let him go!

PEASANT

Thank you! I can finally see my family!

(PEASANT *runs off and* PHIL *goes to stand
with the other guards, grumbling.*)

TAD

But great job, Phil!

ERNEST

Now what do you say we celebrate your return! Let's go get
some dinner!

FRED

Us too?

ERNEST

Of course!

FRED

Excellent!

(Everyone exits but TAD. *He speaks to the audience.)*

TAD

I don't know what it is. I'm so glad to be human, glad to be back and half-ruling the kingdom, but. Suddenly I'm lonely. Ernest and Sylvia have each other. Fred is with Helen. Who do I have?

*(*FRED *and* HELEN *enter.)*

HELEN

Tad, come *on.*

TAD

I'll see you in a bit. I think I'm going to take a little walk.

HELEN

Don't take too long!

*(*FRED *and* HELEN *exit.* TAD *smiles.)*

TAD

At least I still have my friends.

*(*TAD *exits.)*

MILDRED

Phil, you're an inspiration to us all.

PHIL

I think it's time for me to retire.

(Lights fade.)

Scene 11

(The royal pond. TAD enters, bouncing a golden ball. He sits on a bench near the pond and mopes.)

TAD

So, what do *you* think, Mr. Ball? What should I do now? I've got a whole kingdom to co-run but nobody to share it with. I mean I have friends now, and that's kind of a new thing for me, at least friends that are not legally obliged to be my friend, and that's neat. But that's not the *same*.

(He bounces the ball badly and it lands in the pond.)

TAD

And now I don't even have a ball to talk to!

(TAD flops onto the ground pathetically. A LADY FROG enters, out of breath. She spots TAD.)

LADY FROG

Oh, good, a person! *(Approaching TAD.)* Excuse me?

TAD

Aaaaah! A talking frog! Oh, wait.

LADY FROG

Yes, I'm a princess from a neighboring land. A witch turned me into a frog to teach me a lesson. You seemed sad when I approached. Is everything okay?

(TAD looks at LADY FROG in amazement and then turns his head and looks at the audience in disbelief. Blackout.)

THE END